GENESIS

SEVEN LIFE-CHANGING ENCOUNTERS WITH THE GOD OF NEW BEGINNINGS

DR. ALLEN HUNT

 Dynamic Catholic

wellspring

Unless otherwise noted, Scripture passages
have been taken from the *Revised Standard
Version, Catholic Edition*. Copyright 1946, 1952, 1971 by the Division of
Christian Education of the National Council of Churches of Christ in the
USA. Used by permission. All rights reserved.

Quotes are taken from the English translation of the
Catechism of the Catholic Church for the United States of America
(indicated as *CCC*), 2nd ed. Copyright 1997 by United States Catholic
Conference—Libreria Editrice Vaticana.

ISBN: 978-1-63582-273-1

Designed by: Hannah Steen

10 9 8 7 6 5 4 3 2 1

FIRST EDITION

Printed in the United States of America

For Allen, Sam, Matthew, Michael, Betsy,
Mary Grace, and Anna Claire

Seven Beautiful Creations,
Each Made in the Image of God

Table of Contents

ABOUT THE AUTHOR

Dr. Allen Hunt is a best-selling author and nationally acclaimed Catholic Bible teacher.

Allen earned degrees from Mercer University and Emory University, before earning a Ph.D. in New Testament and Ancient Christian Origins from Yale University. His teaching experience includes St. Leo University, as well as at the Pontifical Faculty of the Immaculate Conception at the Dominican House of Studies in Washington, D.C.

In 2008. Allen entered the Catholic Church. This transition represented the culmination of a fifteen-year journey, which was effected by a group of Dominican sisters at Our Lady of Grace Monastery in Connecticut.
Allen shares much of his journey in his best-selling book, *Confessions of a Mega-Church Pastor: How I Discovered the Hidden Treasures of the Catholic Church.*

As a speaker, Allen inspires "everyday" Catholics to more fully recognize the genius of Catholicism, the role it's meant to play in their lives, and how to share that genius with others.

Allen's books include:
- *The Turning Point: 8 Encounters with Jesus that will Change your Life (A Study of the Gospel of John)*
- *Everybody Needs to Forgive Somebody*
- *Dreams for Your Grandchild: The Hidden Power of a Catholic Grandparent*
- *Nine Words: A Bible Study to Help You Become The-Best-Version-of-Yourself*

Dr. Hunt now partners with Matthew Kelly as Senior Advisor at Dynamic Catholic. The Dynamic Catholic team is dedicated to re-energizing the Catholic Church in America by developing world-class resources that inspire people to rediscover the genius of Catholicism.

Allen and his wife, Anita, live in Georgia. Their family includes two daughters, two sons-in-law, and seven grandchildren. For more information, feel free to visit **www.DrAllenHunt.com** and **www.DynamicCatholic.com**.

I am excited to share this time with you as together we discover the beauty of Genesis.

As you study and read, you will begin to see God at work all around you, in everyday life.

Please know that I am praying for you as you seek the presence of our Lord in your study.

May His grace and love abound in your life.

Allen

STUDY OVERVIEW

KEY VERSE:
In the beginning God created the
heavens and the earth....
(Genesis 1:1)

01

GENESIS:

Introduction

Welcome to Genesis—a whole new way to encounter the hand of God in your life. This is the beginning...literally. The very first book of the Bible. The beginning of the world. The start of all human history. It's all right here.

God speaks the world into existence. Then He calls a special people to be His own faithful nation. This is the beginning of life and the beginning of God's people.

This first book of the Bible will have some names and images you know quite well. Genesis shares familiar people—Adam and Eve, Cain and Abel, Noah. And familiar stories that form the foundation of our faith—Creation, the Garden of Eden, the flood and the ark.

They all point toward what is to come in Jesus and the New Testament. These stories provide the basic building blocks for your faith.

A famous book used to say, "Everything I need to know I learned in kindergarten." But the truth may really be, "Everything I need to know I can learn in Genesis."

Genesis was written to teach us how to live. To show us who we are. To tell you the story of where we come from and where we are going. To help you experience the One who made you in His own image.

NOTE: Since participants often do not receive the Study Guide until the first gathering, there is no advance reading assigned to prepare for this first session. The Group Leader will lay the foundation for the study and then lead the group in the discussion questions and video viewing included at the end of this overview. Before preparing for session 2, you will want to read this first lesson on your own in order to have a better understanding of Genesis.

From the start, it's important to understand that Genesis is more concerned with the WHY and the WHO of history than with the HOW and the WHAT of history. Its goal is more to lead you to God than to produce a scientific log book record of events.

Genesis focuses on the big questions of life. Questions like: Where do we come from? Where are we going? What is our origin? Is the universe governed by chance and blind fate, or by a transcendent, intelligent and good Being called "God"? The same questions we find in the Catechism (see 282, 284).

This book is raw with human nature in all its glory and all its darkness. In many ways, Genesis is a single miniature version of the entire Old Testament. And it paves the way for Jesus and God's great promises of the New Testament. When it comes to encountering God and his dream for your life, Genesis is the perfect place to begin.

Genesis is designed to help you get to know God, the One who spoke you and me into existence. He is the Lord, Creator and Ruler of the World. How well do you know Him? Do you want to get to know Him better? Have you ever really encountered Him? Have you been waiting a long time to do so?

In this study, we'll explore seven life-changing encounters the people of Genesis had with the God of new beginnings. We'll discover how these incredible stories reveal the essential foundations of a life of faith. But most importantly, **we will seek to personally encounter the hand of God and see how He is at work all around us in our daily lives.**

As we begin, it is important to realize that you may experience the presence and power of God in a number of ways in this study:

- Through your own personal preparation for each session,
- Through the discussion time in your group, and
- Through watching the video presentation in each lesson.

Are you ready to encounter the God of new beginnings?

Our Process

In our time together, we will study and discuss seven powerful stories in the first half of Genesis (Chapters 1-25). These stories provide the foundation for all we believe. They tell us who we are. They also introduce us to sin and the darker side of ourselves. Best of all, they root us in the marvelous, loving promises of God. He desires great things for your life. And Genesis will help you begin to experience that.

Here is the recommended way for you to prepare for each week:

I. *Your Personal Preparation for the Group Session*

Each week, you will have a reading assignment from the book of Genesis. Using this in preparation for the group session will deepen your own overall understanding and experience of Genesis.

You will read and study the details of one story. Your weekly preparation for the group gathering (Sections I, II, and III) will guide you to reflect on this story.

Each group session will then focus on that story from Genesis to help you dive deeper. Remember we are working to study each story and person in order to enrich our own relationship with the Lord.

In preparation for the weekly group sessions, please complete the appropriate section of the Study Guide on your own. You will find it helpful to set aside about fifteen minutes each day to work on the Study Guide.

Completion of each week's full section of the Study Guide will take about ninety minutes. You will quickly discover that the more intentionally and thoroughly you prepare, the more rewarding your experience will be. God will honor your work and touch your life in new ways.

We suggest you begin your preparation and reading time each day with prayer. Ask God to open your eyes, ears, and heart to His voice in Sacred Scripture as you read. Then make this simple request: "Lord, please open my eyes to how you are at work in this story and at work in my life."

End your time of preparation with prayer. The Prayer of a Dynamic Catholic (found on the inside back cover) is the suggested way to do this.

II. Group Session (approximately 60 minutes)

You will need your Study Guide and Bible for each group session.

1. **Gathering and Announcements** (5 minutes)

2. **Opening Group Prayer** (5 minutes)
    Prayer by St. Richard of Chichester (found on the inside front cover)

3. **Watch Video and use the Response Sheet for notes** (20 minutes).

4. **Small Group Discussion** (25 minutes)
    Study Guide and Readings
    Prayer and Encouragement

5. **Closing Prayer** (5 minutes)
    Prayer of a Dynamic Catholic (found on the inside back cover)

III. Resources

- *Genesis: Seven Life-Changing Encounters with the God of New Beginnings*
- Bible (suggested version: Revised Standard Version, Catholic Edition)

NOTE: *All Scripture references in this study are from the Revised Standard Version, Catholic Edition (RSV-CE), unless otherwise noted. The study's author has chosen to capitalize references to the name of God in the translation printed in the study guide.*

Setting and Style

The book of Genesis overflows with rich treasures. This great book sits squarely at the beginning of the Christian Bible but also at the beginning of what Jewish tradition calls the Torah ("Teaching" or "Law"). The Torah, comprised of the first five books of the Old Testament, contains the basic core teaching of the Jewish faith. These five prestigious and sacred books share the story of the formation of Israel, the people of God. And they provide the blueprint for understanding the rest of Sacred Scripture.

Beginnings are important. Genesis launches the story of God and His relationship with humanity. It sets the stage for all that is to come. That's part of the reason the first word of Genesis is the Hebrew word for *"In the beginning…"*

Genesis does not provide the end of the story, just the beginning. This book sets the stage for the next book (Exodus) where Moses and the people of Israel in bondage in Egypt wait for their God to deliver them into the land that has been promised all the way back in **Genesis 12** to Abraham.

Ancient Jews, and much of Judaism today, credit Moses for writing the Torah. Scholars and traditions today like to debate whether Moses is the author, or whether Genesis represents the work of multiple sources and traditions. Regardless, we know that Moses regularly taught the people the contents of this book and all that follows. And people of faith have been using it in powerful ways ever since.

Genesis focuses more on communicating God's love and the purpose of life than on precisely recording details as if they were in a courtroom. It is important to remember that ancient history focused more on WHY something happened than WHAT exactly occurred.

Thus, Genesis provides seven essential foundations of the life of faith. In sharing the story of history, this book helps us know who we are and how to live. We begin to see God at work all around us every day as Genesis roots us in these foundations:

a. **GOODNESS:** God Creates the Good World and Treasures Human Life
b. **SIN:** Humans are Messy and so is Life
c. **FREE WILL:** Life is Choices
d. **NEW BEGINNINGS:** God Punishes, but He Also Forgives
e. **COVENANT:** God has a Special Sacred Bond with His People
f. **FAITHFULNESS:** God Makes and Honors His Bold Promises
g. **FAITH and TRUST:** We Can Partner with God

These themes provide the opportunity for you to encounter our living God in the same way the great people of Genesis did.

When we do so, we discover who we are. We learn how to live the way God desires. Best of all, the Genesis stories are so powerful that we can keep coming back to them over and over in our own lives. Their truth is timeless. And that truth can guide you through every turn and decision of life.

No matter what has happened in your past, no matter what challenges you face today, the dream God has for your future begins right here.

Layout

Overall, Genesis can be divided into four large sections. Each of these four sections builds upon the one before it to slowly reveal the story of the people Israel. In this study, we will focus on the first two large sections (I and II below).

I. THE BEGINNING: Chapters 1-11

God creates the world and human beings, who tend to sin.

II. ABRAHAM: Chapters 12-25

God blesses and calls Abraham, and then makes a bold promise to all of Abraham's descendants.

III. ISAAC and JACOB: Chapters 26-36

The son and grandson of Abraham carry on and live into the special blessing given by God.

IV. JOSEPH: Chapters 37-50

The powerful story of Joseph shares how he ends up in Egypt, and how God uses Joseph's life to set the stage for all that will happen for the people of Israel in the Exodus.

Throughout Genesis, we will see how God works with human beings, and sometimes in spite of them, to accomplish His purpose. We will meet God powerfully and personally. And we will work to resist our own sinfulness in order to enter into the bold future He has planned from the very beginning.

SESSION ONE:

INTRODUCTORY GROUP SESSION

Video Response Sheet

KEY VERSE:

In the beginning God created the heavens and the earth.....
(1:1)

Fill in the blanks and take notes as we watch the video together.

1. Beginnings are _____.

2. For the Jews, this is _____.

    a. _____

    b. First _____ books

    c. _____

3. _____ more than _____

    a. Ancient History focuses mostly on communicating
    _____ and _____.

SOMETHING OLD, SOMETHING NEW

(Connecting Genesis with the New Testament and the Genius of our Catholic Faith)

God, infinitely perfect and blessed in himself, in a plan of sheer goodness freely created man to make him share in his own blessed life.

For this reason, at every time and in every place, God draws close to man.

He calls man to seek him, to know him, to love him with all his strength.

He calls together all men, scattered and divided by sin, into the unity of his family, the Church.

(CCC 1)

NOTE: *A "Something Old, Something New" page appears after each lesson. It is designed to help you connect the dots between what we are discovering together in Genesis with what comes later in the Bible in the New Testament and becomes an important foundation of our Catholic faith. It is designed for your personal use but can certainly be included in group discussions if desired.*

SESSION ONE:

INTRODUCTORY GROUP SESSION

Beginning the Journey Together

GROUP SHARING

1. **Who are you?** Share your name and one thing about yourself no one else in the room knows. (e.g., a hobby, a guilty pleasure you enjoy, or a funny detail from your past)

2. **Why are you here?** What are your hopes for this study and the group sessions?

3. **What one area of your life do you hope is most impacted by studying the Book of Genesis?**

4. **What will you plan to do to make sure you get the most out of this experience?**

   Envision your place to study Genesis and prepare for each session. Is it your kitchen table, or your favorite chair or a familiar desk?

   Set in your mind the time you plan to be in that place to study. Will it be early in the morning? A late night appointment? Your lunch break?

JOURNAL

How is life? Reflect on what's working and what's not working in your life.

Consider your hopes, your fears, your relationships, your work, your finances, your dreams, and your emotions. Write down your thoughts about how your life is working right now.

The Creator has answers to your questions. He offers you the best way to live. Together we will seek Him in our preparation and in these sessions. We will pray for one another and encourage each other forward. May our journeys be filled with His grace.

DEEPEN YOUR GENESIS EXPERIENCE

FREE ACCESS to 8 inspiring companion videos on Dynamic+ featuring Allen Hunt. Scan the code to the left to watch now or visit **dynamiccatholic.com/genesis**

"When it comes to encountering God and his dream for your life, Genesis is the perfect place to begin."

— ALLEN HUNT

For Next Time

Please read and complete the Session 2 Study Guide and answer the questions.

At the next session, we will discuss the Study Guide questions and watch the Session 2 Video.

NOTE: Please bring your completed Session Two Study Guide and your Bible to the next group session.

YOU ARE MADE WITH LOVE IN THE IMAGE OF GOD

KEY VERSE:
And God saw everything that He had made, and behold, it was very good.
(Genesis 1:31)

02

I. Laying the Foundation

READ: GENESIS 1:1-2:4

This is it. The beginning of the entire universe. God creates something out of nothing. Even better, He creates the entire world out of sheer nothingness.

God doesn't need any help. He doesn't even need raw materials. Nothing is impossible with our Lord.

In fact, the Lord *speaks* Creation into existence. You'll notice in this story that Genesis says He "*creates*" several times; it says He "*makes*" five times; but God "*speaks*" <u>fourteen</u> times. Our God can simply speak reality into existence. God speaks; all Creation listens and responds.

By speaking, the Lord makes something come out of nothing. In the world around us, that just does not happen. Something always has to come from something else. But that is how powerful our Lord is. He can speak something out of nothing. Nothing is impossible for Him.

And God is very pleased with His work. When the Lord looks at all He has created, He sees that it is all "very good." He has created a very good world to show His glory and goodness. After all, God is love.

Best of all, the Lord saves His most special work for His final act of creation. On the sixth day of Creation, God *speaks* human beings into existence. He creates us in His own image. He breathes His own life into us. And then the Lord does one more thing: He blesses human life.

In other words, you are made with love. And with goodness. God's breath flows within you. He made you because that's what Love does: it creates. Your life is no accident. When God made you, He had a purpose in mind for your life. And He still desires to help you find and fulfill that purpose.

God loves you just because you are. Your life matters because you were made by God Himself. You belong to Him.

Remarkably, the Lord made you in His very own image. That means your life is sacred. It has value. You have been made by love and with love. It is hard to believe, but you look a lot like God.

What may be even harder to believe is that all the people around you are valuable too. They are loved. Because they too were hand-crafted by God. He spoke every single one of us into existence.

God is good, and so is His Creation. After all, everything has come from Him. He is the source of it all. God is love.

And God begins His loving relationship with us humans right here in the beginning of the Bible, in **Genesis 1**. From this point on, everything that happens will tell the story of God's goodness and His love, of His hopes for human beings and His dreams for our lives.

Creation, prepare to meet the good, loving Lord: Father, Son and Holy Spirit.

If God had drawn the world from pre-existent matter, what would be so extraordinary in that? A human artisan makes from a given material whatever he wants, while God shows His power by starting from nothing to make all He wants.

ST. THEOPHILUS OF ANTIOCH

II. This Week's Encounter
GENESIS 1:1-2:4

These first chapters of Genesis set up the entire Bible. These verses describe a God who made us in His own image. A God who created us for a relationship with Himself. This is who we are!

Answer the following questions to help you reflect on what you read in these verses from Genesis. **TIP: Circle the questions you find the most interesting or difficult and discuss them with your group at the next session.**

1. **Genesis 1:1** starts with *"In the beginning..."* This verse not only starts the book of Genesis, it also starts the entire Bible. In fact, this verse starts the creation of the world. Compare that to the **Gospel of John 1:1**:

    "In the beginning was the Word,
    and the Word was with God,
    and the Word was God."

    Why do you think John chooses to use that same phrase from Genesis when he begins to introduce us to Jesus in his Gospel?

    _____

    _____

    _____

    _____

    _____

    _____

2. Reading these verses of **Genesis 1** is much like watching a time-sequence video. Seven days of creation unfold before your eyes. Slowly and steadily, God brings order out of chaos. He brings light out of the darkness. He creates the whole universe out of nothing.

Close your eyes and have someone read these days below aloud to you. Envision in your mind's eye as each day's work of Creation occurs.

Day 1 *Heaven and earth - night and day* **(1:1-5)**
Day 2 *Sky* **(1:6-8)**
Day 3 *Vegetation and seas – earth and water* **(1:9-13)**
Day 4 *Planets and stars, the sun and the moon* **(1:14-19)**
Day 5 *Sea dwellers and birds of the air* **(1:20-23)**
Day 6 *Living creatures on earth and humankind* **(1:24-31)**
Day 7 *Sabbath* **(2:1-3)**

This flow says something about God. Like the conductor of a symphony, He masterfully orchestrates the existence of all that is. God creates carefully, not in some casual or accidental fashion. Hear the swell of the musical crescendo as the Creation comes into being all the way to its climax with God's final masterpiece, human beings, like you and me.

Notice how the pattern of each day of Creation mirrors the one before.

TIME: Evening and morning
ACTION: God said, "Let there be..."
RESULT: And it was
EVALUATION: God saw that it was good
TIME: There was evening and morning

The design of the world is not accidental. Things happen precisely upon God's command. God has a purpose and a will for Creation. In fact, that's the only reason it exists in the first place.

Does this story help you sense the nearness of God? Or do you more stand back with awe and wonder at His majesty and the grandeur of His work?

----

3. Our key verse for this session is:

    "And God saw everything that He had made,
    and behold, it was very good."
    (Genesis 1:31)

    Have you heard this verse before?

    Notice how **Genesis 1** declares time and again that God's creation is "good."

    READ:
    1:4, 1:10, 1:12, 1:18, 1:21, 1:25, and 1:31

    Clearly, God sees the world as His special treasure.

    We often see the world as bad. But that's not so. There is certainly evil in the world, but people of faith see the great capacity for good in the world and in the people around us.

All Creation comes from God's goodness and love. This means that you are loved simply for who you are.

Is it challenging or easy for you to see other people as good, as being made in the image of God just like you are?

_____

_____

_____

_____

_____

_____

Why do you think that is?

_____

_____

_____

_____

_____

4. A most special part of our faith comes from **Genesis 1**. Notice the unique relationship and role God has in mind for us human beings. The Lord has big dreams and large expectations for us. After all, we are His masterpiece.

a. **Verses 1:26-27** remind us three times that humans are made in the **image of God**. We resemble the One who created us.

That means human life has deep, sacred value. It is the only part of Creation explicitly said to have been made in the image of God. In a way, you and I are little images of God in the world.

This special value has real significance for how we live. Each life has sacred value. It is why the Church teaches the value of life from conception all the way to natural death.

What does it mean to you that all human beings are made in the image of God?

How might this change how you interact with people who annoy you or people you find to be difficult? Or how might this value change how you treat a stranger?

Read Colossians 3:7-14. What do these verses say about how the image of God is revealed in how we live and behave?

_____

_____

_____

_____

_____

b. He not only makes us human beings in His image, God also **blesses human life**. Look at **Genesis 1:28**.

c. The Lord **speaks directly** to human beings in **1:28-30**. We are the only part of Creation with that special relationship with Him. We can freely respond to the sound of God's voice.

d. God also places humans at the **top of Creation's organizational chart**. How would you describe what God instructs humans to do in **1:27-30**?

_____

_____

_____

_____

_____

5. **Look at Genesis 2:1-3.** These verses describe the seventh day, the culmination of Creation. The Sabbath.

God does not spend the Sabbath in exhaustion but rather in serenity and peace. Notice how He blesses His work and especially calls the seventh day "Holy." Here God gives us the mode for the Sabbath as a regular, consistent day of rest.

Read Exodus 20:8-11. God establishes that same Sabbath as one of the ten commandments.

How do you practice the Sabbath?

In a busy world, with twenty-four hour, seven days a week stores and schedules, it can be challenging to remember the importance of what God teaches us here: rest, reflection, worship, and gratitude. These help restore us and keep us fresh.

What one or two ways might you allow the Sabbath to impact your own life and your relationship with God more powerfully?

Take a moment to breathe in a Sabbath prayer like one of these:

————————————

What we need most in order to make progress,
Is to be silent before this great God
With our appetite, and with our tongue,
For the language He best hears is silent love.

ST. JOHN OF THE CROSS

————————————

My life is an instant,
a fleeting hour.
My life is a moment,
which swiftly escapes me.
O my God, you know that
on earth I have only today
to love you.

ST. THERESE OF LISIEUX

————————————

You are indeed Holy, O Lord,
And all you have created
Rightly gives you praise

EUCHARISTIC PRAYER III

III. *Just for You: Experiencing God*

This section will not be discussed in the group setting. It is designed specifically to help grow your own personal relationship with God.

1. Look at **1 John 4:7-8**
    and **1 John 4:19**

    What do these verses say about who God is?

    _____

    _____

    _____

    _____

    _____

    Remember that you are made in His image. What does that mean for who God intends you to be?

    _____

    _____

    _____

    _____

    _____

2. Now look at **Mark 12:28-34**

What does Jesus say are the two key parts of the greatest commandment?

----

3. In other words,

God is **Love**

And you are made in His image, the image of **Love**

So, God designed you to love Him and to love the people around you because they are made in that same image of **Love**.

We love because we were made **IN Love, BY Love, in order TO Love**.

4. Rank yourself on a scale of 1 to 10 regarding how well you are doing with:

LOVING GOD	1	2	3	4	5	6	7	8	9	10
	LOW								HIGHEST	
LOVING PEOPLE	1	2	3	4	5	6	7	8	9	10

5. What one step might you take to love people a little bit more this week?

Remember each person is made in the image of God.

Here are four possible next steps. Pick one of these or craft one of your own to do this week.

- When an annoying person crosses your path, pause and say to yourself, "You are made in the image of God. You are worthy of grace just like I am."

- Spend time visiting in person or by phone with an elderly friend or family member who is shut in, ill, or living alone.

- Give an hour of your time, or make a gift, to a pregnancy resource center to help love and protect the life of an unborn child.

- Volunteer in a food pantry or a clothing closet ministry to provide comfort to a person in need of life's basics.

SESSION TWO:
VIDEO RESPONSE SHEET

Fill in the blanks and take notes as we watch the video together.

1. It's all about _____

"And God saw everything that He had made,
and behold,
it was very good."
(Genesis 1:31)

3. The _____ of _____

I was born to a woman I never knew.
I was raised by a woman who took in children.
I don't know my lineage, my heritage, or my roots.
So when I meet someone new, I treat them with respect.
After all, they could be my people.

ATTRIBUTED TO JAMES MICHENER

JOURNAL AND NOTES

SOMETHING OLD, SOMETHING NEW

(Connecting Genesis with the New Testament and the Genius of our Catholic Faith)

Since God could create everything out of nothing,

he can also, through the Holy Spirit,

give spiritual life to sinners by creating a pure heart in them

and bodily life to the dead through the Resurrection.

(CCC 298)

———————

The same Spirit

that brought life into existence

desires to bring new life to

your heart and soul.

———————

For Next Time

Please read and complete the Session 3 Study Guide and answer the questions.

At the next session, we will discuss the Study Guide questions and watch the Session 3 Video.

NOTE: Please bring your completed Session 3 Study Guide and your Bible to the next group session.

HUMANS ARE MESSY, AND SO IS LIFE

KEY VERSE:
For God knows that when you eat of it your eyes will be opened, and you will be like God, knowing good and evil. (Genesis 3:5)

03

I. Laying the Foundation

READ: GENESIS 2:4-3:24

Adam and Eve. The Garden of Eden. The serpent. The tree of life. Forbidden fruit. Disobedience. The aftershocks of their choice. **Genesis 2 and 3** lay out the raw naked truth for everyone to see.

These verses share the intimate details about the beginning of human existence. We experience the first human misbehavior and its disastrous results. This story reveals the foundations of what we have come to call "Original Sin."

God makes the universe, creates the first man, and places him in paradise. Adam names all the animals. But God notices in **2:18** that Adam is lonely and needs a companion. So He makes Adam a "helper." Eve becomes a source of strength to partner with Adam in life.

But the partnership quickly takes a turn in a direction God does not desire. The serpent tempts Eve, inviting her to taste forbidden fruit and *"be like God."* The seeds of sin are planted. Adam and Eve do exactly what God instructs them not to do. They turn away from Him and choose to go their own way. That's what sin is. Turning away from God.

Make no mistake. Satan knows that the easiest way to shortchange your vision and your life from God is to tempt you to go your own way. He encourages you to focus on your own appetites, urges, and conveniences. Satan wants to create distance between you and God.

Sin causes us to push God aside and to put ourselves and our own desires first. Pride is the deadliest of all life-killers. In the dictionary, "pride" is first defined as a healthy self-worth and confidence. That's a good thing. But the next definition for pride is a "preoccupation with self." And that's not so good.

Pride is the father of all the other sins. C.S. Lewis said that pride is spiritual cancer, a complete anti-God state of mind. We know it as "All about me" disease. Again, it is a turning away from God.

No matter what you call it – pride is putting yourself where God should be: at the center of life. When you place anything other than God at the center, life begins to go wrong. And it starts right here in the beginning with Adam, Eve and the Garden.

Unfortunately, you and I often do the same thing. We turn away from God. When we do, we experience distance from Him. And that's when things begin to go wrong in our lives.

Adam and Eve, prepare to meet the Lord, rightful center of our lives.

_____

By his sin, Adam, as the first man, lost the original holiness and justice he had received from God,
not only for himself but for all human beings.

Adam and Eve transmitted to their descendants human nature wounded by their own first sin and hence deprived of original holiness and justice;
this deprivation is called "original sin."

(CCC 416-417)

II. This Week's Encounter

GENESIS 2:4-3:24

These verses share intimate details about the beginning of human life and the first human disobedience. Adam and Eve display the same kind of struggles we all face.

Answer the following questions to help you reflect on what you have read in these verses from Genesis. **TIP: Circle the questions you find most interesting or difficult and discuss them with your group at the next session.**

1. **Read Genesis 2:4-14.** Take a moment and close your eyes. Envision each of these steps in the Creation story taking place. See the sights, smell the smells, hear the noises as God creates. Watch in awe as.....

    - Mist comes up from the earth and waters the whole face of the ground
    - God picks up dust from the earth and forms the first man
    - God breathes breath into that first man's nostrils, and he becomes a living soul
    - God plants a garden in Eden
    - Trees begin to grow from the earth, and fruit fills their branches
    - A river flows out of Eden and waters the garden

    How do you feel as you experience God creating life? What strikes you? What emotion(s) do you experience?

Look again at 2:7

> *"...then the Lord God formed man of dust from the ground,*
> *and breathed into his nostrils the breath of life;*
> *and man became a living soul."*

Read also **Isaiah 64:8** and **Romans 9:21**

Observe how God is like a potter, forming the first human out of the dust of the earth. Notice how God is the life-giver, animating those humans with His own breath of life.

Have you ever crafted something with your hands that you felt particularly good about or proud of?

Can you remember times in your own life when God has formed and shaped you like a potter does the earth? Forming you into something new?

How might God be at work right now in your life to shape you into the vessel or shape He desires? Do you sense His hand forming you?

----

2. **Read Genesis 2:15-17**. Remember from the previous session that God puts human beings at the top of Creation's organizational chart. He instructs us to care for Creation, to exercise control over it, and to be fruitful and multiply. Here in **Genesis 2**, more details emerge. God instructs the first humans to till and keep the Garden of Eden, and to eat freely from every tree there, except for the tree of the knowledge of good and evil.

God tries to be clear about what He expects us to do and to not do. He not only does that here with the first humans, He also does it for everyone in the ten commandments.

Take a look at **Exodus 20:3-17**. Write down a few things God instructs us to be sure to do. And write down a few things He clearly teaches us not to do.

DO   **NOT DO**

3. **Read Genesis 2:18-25**. As God looks at Adam, He realizes that one human being will be lonely, that human beings need the company or companionship of other human beings. So God creates a partner, or helper.

   The word for "helper" here does not mean "servant." In fact, it's the same word often used to describe God in the Scriptures.

   "My soul waits for the Lord, my HELP and my shield"
   (Ps. 33:20)

   "The Lord is my HELP and my deliverer"
   (Ps. 70:5)

   Notice how God takes a rib from Adam and fashions it into the first woman. The first two human beings come from the same substance and flesh just as they will be joined together as one flesh in marriage. They are true partners in flesh and also in name as Adam calls her the Hebrew "ishshah" for woman, a word formed from the Hebrew "ish" for man.

4. Our key verse for this session is:

   "For God knows that when you eat of it your eyes will be opened, and you will be like God, knowing good and evil."
   (Genesis 3:5)

   Read Genesis 3:1-7. Notice how the serpent does not lie but twists the truth to create envy and temptation. "You will be like God." The serpent manipulates the truth first to tempt Eve, and then to tempt Adam.

Eve takes the fruit, inspects it and rationalizes all the way to the first bite. She then shares it with Adam who does the same. They are both willing participants in disobeying God. With that disobedience, Paradise is lost.

This is the central event. Enter sin and its far-reaching aftershocks.

Both Adam and Eve are willing participants in sin. Aren't we all? The serpent tempts, and we give in to urges and desires that lead us away from God. This is how Satan works in our lives. When we seek to find satisfaction outside of God, we wander away.

Write down a few times when you have been tempted this week to do the wrong rather than the right.

Can you remember times in your life when you intentionally tempted someone else to do the wrong thing?

Times when someone else tempted you?

----

5. Notice in **Genesis 3:6-7** how the eyes lead Adam and Eve astray. Their eyes lead straight from temptation into sin. Our eyes can get us in real trouble if we are not careful.

We fall into sin when we seek to be completely free from God and to place ourselves squarely in charge. When we resist praying because we think we can handle life on our own. When we fail to ask for God's help or direction and choose to make plans all by ourselves. When we view everything as "my time, my money, my body, my pleasure, my comfort, my decision." We try to secure our own well-being without God. And that simply is not possible.

Clearly, sin is real and has been a problem for us humans since the very beginning. Adam and Eve were destined to live with God, but failed to accept God's terms. They are cast out of the Garden. That is what sin does: it separates us from God.

For more on how our eyes, left unguarded, can lead into sin, take a look at

Genesis 12:14-15   **Numbers 15:37-41**   **2 Samuel 11:2-5**

6. In **Genesis 3:8-11**, God already knows what Adam and Eve have done, but He asks them about it anyway. God seeks the truth in order to get their confession. He knows that speaking the truth is the first step toward healing our souls.

   Notice how they play the "Blame Game" in **Gen. 3:12-13**. Adam blames Eve and then God Himself. Eve blames the serpent. It's an easy game to play.

   Can you think of a time this week when you have fallen into the "blame game" instead of simply accepting responsibility for your misstep or stumbling?

   Have you ever felt relief in confessing something you were trying to hide?

Does **Genesis 3:8-11** make you feel differently about the sacrament of Confession/Reconciliation?

_____

_____

_____

_____

_____

_____

> *The eye through which I see God*
> *is the same eye through which God sees me;*
> *my eye and God's eye are one eye, one seeing,*
> *one knowing, one love.*
>
> **Meister Eckhardt**

III. Just for You: Experiencing God

This section will not be discussed in the group setting. It is designed specifically to help grow your own personal relationship with God.

1. Sin possesses a strong tug in each of us. None of us wants to turn away from God. Yet, we regularly find ourselves wandering off on our own into our own paths and desires.

    Where do you most often find temptation in your own life? What kinds of people, events, places or desires are most likely to lure you into turning away from God's hopes for you? Do you see an area of your life where you particularly lack contentment?

    When you consider the 7 deadly sins, circle the one that seems to possess the greatest temptation power in your own life?

    Pride   Anger   Greed   Gluttony   Lust   Envy   Sloth

2. Think about the areas of your life: your family, relationships, work, emotional well-being, financial stability, spiritual life, and so on. What factors in these areas most often lead to your own temptation or even stumbling into sin? Again, do you lack contentment? Can you see one or two specific things that are likely to cause you the most harm? Name them truthfully. In doing so, you can claim God's power to give you the strength to resist temptation.

Examine these three steps to strengthen yourself against temptation and increase your level of contentment. Implement one of these steps this week. Embrace freedom from the power of sin in your life.

1. Don't take yourself too seriously. Laugh at yourself at least once a day. Take a deep breath when you find yourself being too serious about your own importance or trying to play the blame game.

2. Put God on your calendar. Schedule a few minutes each day this week to talk with Him. Use **Psalm 51** in your prayer life to gain words of strength.

3. Ask God to bring to your mind the sins you need to confess. Make use of the powerful Sacrament of Confession/Reconciliation. Speaking the truth can give new strength to your mind, body and soul.

SESSION THREE:
VIDEO RESPONSE SHEET

KEY VERSE:

For God knows that when you eat of it your eyes will be opened, and you will be like God, knowing good and evil.

(Genesis 3:5)

Fill in the blanks and take notes as we watch the video together.

1. DED = _____

   - When the eyes lead astray
   - Deadly

2. DED blinds you

   - From seeing _____
   - To _____ in your life
   - To _____

3. The cure for DED = _____

"Not that I complain of want; for I have learned,
in whatever state I am, to be content.
I know how to be abased, and I know how to abound.
In any and all circumstances I have learned
the secret facing plenty and hunger, abundance and want.
I can do all things in him who strengthens me."
(Philippians 4:11-13)

JOURNAL AND NOTES

SOMETHING OLD, SOMETHING NEW

(Connecting Genesis with the New Testament and the Genius of our Catholic Faith)

"For as in Adam all die, so also in Christ shall all be made alive."
(1 Cor. 15:22)

———————

Jesus Christ is God's solution

to the problem Adam and Eve created.

———————

For Next Time

Please read and complete the Session 4 Study Guide and answer the questions.

At the next session, we will discuss the Study Guide questions and watch the Session 4 Video.

NOTE: Please bring your completed Session 4 Study Guide and your Bible to the next group session.

LIFE IS CHOICES

KEY VERSE:
And when they were in the field, Cain
rose up against his brother, Abel, and
killed him.
(Genesis 4:8b)

04

I. Laying the Foundation

READ: GENESIS 4:1-16

Adam and Eve found it hard to live on God's terms in the Garden of Eden. But we're about to discover that living with other human beings is even tougher.

Adam and Eve have two sons, Cain and Abel. Both bring their sacrifice, their personal offering, to God. However, the Lord accepts only one. God looks with favor on Abel but not on Cain. This is a difficult and painful story. The stories in Genesis can be hard.

Genesis doesn't make plain the exact reason why God is pleased only with Abel's offering. The story focuses mostly on Cain's reaction.

When the brothers go out to the field, Cain attacks Abel and kills him. Envy resents the blessings other people enjoy. Cain allows his raging bloodlust to overwhelm, and he chooses to act with violence. Anger and jealousy lead to murder.

Life is choices. This is one of life's greatest truths and its hardest lesson. It is a great truth, because it reminds us of our power. Not power over others, but the often-untapped power to be ourselves and to live the life we have imagined. It is a hard lesson, because it causes us to realize that our choices have in some way brought about the life we are living right now. It is perhaps frightening for us to think that we have chosen our life as it is today. Frightening because we may not like what we find when we look at our lives today. But it is also liberating, because we can now begin to choose what we find when we look at our life in the tomorrows that lie unlived before us.

What will you see when you look at yourself and your life ten years from now? What will you choose?

Every day you make hundreds of choices. What to eat. What time to arrive. Who to spend time with. What to care about. Many of these choices may seem inconsequential. But one choice builds upon another, and in the end our choices define who we become.

Love is a choice. Anger is a choice. Gratitude is a choice. Fear is a choice. Courage is a choice. You choose.

Sometimes we choose the-best-version-of-ourselves, and sometimes we choose a-second-rate-version-of-ourselves.

We face choices each day. It can be easy to turn away from God just like Cain did.

In the end, God doesn't let go. The Lord punishes Cain, sending him farther away. Cain finds himself more separated from God spiritually and physically than was ever intended. Cain experiences the painful consequences of his violent choice. Yet, still God's mercy persists. Even in the punishment, God spares Cain's life and protects him. God punishes, God forgives; but most of all, God never abandons.

Our sovereign God creates us free. We each possess the freedom to choose Him and the freedom to walk away from Him. God's love never wavers, even loving us enough to let us decide for ourselves and experience the consequences of those choices.

Children of the Garden, prepare to meet the God of free will.

II. This Week's Encounter

GENESIS 4:1-16

These verses share the famous story of Cain and Abel. And that story reveals the power of anger and jealousy, a power so strong that it leads to death. Our choices can lead to life. They can also lead to death.

Answer the following questions to help you reflect on what you read. **TIP: Circle the questions you find the most interesting or difficult and discuss them with your group at the next session.**

1. **Read Gen. 4:1-7.** Notice how both Cain and Abel appear to do what is appropriate. They bring their sacrificial offering to God.

   Both men expect God's acceptance; yet one offering is accepted, and one is not. Again, the reason is not made totally clear.

   This can be a hard lesson to absorb. Life is not always fair. Throughout the book of Genesis, God often disrupts and creates tension. Genesis does not portray some kind of lame, tame, timid God. The Lord certainly does not have to explain Himself to His creation. After all, He is God.

   In much the same way, He has given us freedom to choose what we will do as well. We are made in the image of God, and we all face choices each day. We get to choose

   • how we will live,
   • how we will love,
   • and how we will invest our lives

List one or two moments in your life when you have realized that life is not fair.

_____

_____

_____

_____

_____

Have those moments ever caused you to question God?

_____

_____

_____

_____

_____

2. **Pay attention to verse 7**. Notice

   a) "Do well" – even after the Garden of Eden, humans still can "do well." Each of us can choose and act for good. Free will comes with being a human.

   b) God tells Cain that "sin is lurking at the door." Sin waits like a hungry lion ready to pounce. It is larger than Adam, Eve, Cain or any of us. The opportunity to make poor choices is very, very real. We can choose to turn away from God.

c) God offers a positive warning to sin in **4:7**. "You must master it." Again, we have choices. Free will. Can you think of an area in your life where you struggle with sin and God is calling you to "do well?"

_____

_____

_____

_____

_____

3. **Read St. Paul's words in Romans 7:15-18**

"I do not understand my own actions. For I do not do what I want, but I do the very thing I hate. Now if I do what I do not want, I agree that the law is good. So then it is no longer I that do it, but sin which dwells within me, that is, in my flesh. I can will what is right, but I cannot do it."

These verses from Romans present the real struggle, don't they? We often want to do good and yet still choose not to do it. When have you experienced that?

_____

_____

_____

_____

_____

4. **Read Gen. 4:8-10.** Notice Cain's choice and its consequences. The Scriptures often contrast good choices and bad ones. Consider:

- Abel and Cain, both sons of Adam: Abel chooses God, Cain chooses murder
- Peter and Judas, both deny their Lord: Peter seeks mercy, while Judas seeks death
- Two thieves, both on crosses beside Jesus: one chooses Jesus, the other chooses condemnation

In every age of history, every page of Scripture, God allows us to make our own choices. And to live with the consequences. Often, that is how we learn the most.

Everything is a choice, and our choices echo throughout our lives... and into history... and into eternity. Such is the unfathomable power of God's gift of free will.

We often hear choice spoken of as if it is automatically a good thing. But not all choices are good choices. There is such a thing as a bad choice, and it's important to remind ourselves of that, because the culture is unlikely to. The reason some choices are bad is because there is death in some choices. Your death, the death of others, the death of relationships, the death of the environment, death in all shapes and sizes. We don't always recognize this death because it usually is not complete death. We make choices that bring about a little bit of death and destruction, small deaths, and the point is to choose life in every choice.

What are two really excellent choices you have made?

What did you learn from making one of those choices?

Can you name one really poor decision you made? What factors or forces led you to make that choice?

What did you learn from that poor decision?

----

5. Envy, one of the seven deadly sins, shows its ugly self in the story of Cain
    and Abel. Jealousy provokes anger, which in turns provokes violence. Envy
    drives Cain to commit the first murder in history.

    Envy can start an ugly chain reaction. Left uncontrolled, envy can lead to
    gossip, or to a broken relationship, or to bitterness at another person's
    success. It can lead anywhere but love.

    Can you think of a time when jealousy has caused someone to harm you?

When has envy moved you to make a mistake or treat someone unkindly?

---

6. **Read Gen. 4:11-16.** God is a God of justice. Cain must be punished. He is sentenced to be a fugitive and a wanderer, never to have a land or prosperity of his own.

   Yet, even here, God is still a God of mercy. God asks Cain a question. "Where is your brother Abel?" Again, God knows the answer but is trying to draw out a confession just like He did with Adam and Eve in the Garden.

   God places a mark on Cain. That mark clearly establishes Cain as belonging to God. Much like tattoos used to mark ancient tribes, the mark of God shows who Cain belongs to. Even in sin, Cain still belongs to God. In a way, the mark shows that Cain is also protected by God. It is a mark of grace. God has judged Cain, but nevertheless He will still provide for him.

   Think about the words we say before receiving communion: "Lord, I am not worthy that you should enter under my roof, but only say the word and my soul shall be healed."

What comes to mind when you say these words aloud? Do you believe that, even when you have chosen poorly, God still makes a place for you when you seek to return home?

Does this story cause you to reflect differently on what is happening at that moment in the Eucharist?

----

7. Learning to make great choices is one of the most practical skills you can develop, because decision making is central to everything we do.

Prayer helps us develop the personal clarity necessary to make great choices. It also provides an environment for us to consider the options and opportunities before us each day, rather than trying to make important decisions in the midst of the hustle and bustle of life. Adopting a daily habit of prayer provides an opportunity to pause, reflect, and decide. We call this process discernment.

As we get clear about who we are, what we are here for, what matters most, and what matters least, we get really good at one thing that most people are particularly poor at: saying no.

The heart of being a good decision maker is getting good at saying no. The reality is you get to say yes to very few things compared to the number of things you need to say no to. Life is full of opportunities. Every time you say yes to something you say no to dozens, even hundreds of things. Consider the example of marriage. People get married every day. They think of it as saying yes to a person, but in saying yes to that person, we are also saying no to every other person. In each marriage there is one yes and millions of no's.

When we say yes to things we know are not for us, we miss out on all that God created just for us. And it's those things that God created just for us that we're hungry for, that are worth chasing, that we yearn for.

How much would a father or mother worry about their child if they knew their son or daughter would always make good decisions? If you knew this as a parent, most of your concerns, worries, and fears would be alleviated. This demonstrates how central making good decisions is to our lives.

Life is choices. We are constantly making them. A daily habit of prayer and reflection helps us to discern and choose the good in the situations we encounter in our journey. Only then will we learn to find life in every choice.

III. *Just for You: Experiencing God*

This section will not be discussed in the group setting. It is designed specifically to help grow your own personal relationship with God.

1. Write down two moments from your life when you have felt far away from God. Perhaps a time you felt ignored, even rejected, by God because of what you had done.

    _____

    _____

    _____

    _____

    _____

    _____

2. Were any of these two moments of distance or separation from God a result of consequences of your own poor choices?

    _____

    _____

    _____

    _____

    _____

    _____

3. Prayer helps us develop the personal clarity necessary to make great choices. A habit of daily prayer stimulates better decision. For one week, use one of these prayers below to generate healthier awareness and healthier choices.

   a) The Jesus Prayer, started in the 6th century, as a simple prayer to repeat to bring your soul back into its place with God. Try reciting these words seven times each day this week: when you awaken, at breakfast, mid-morning, at lunch, mid-afternoon, at dinner, and at bedtime. Allow the words to orient your soul with the mercy of God at the center.

   Lord Jesus Christ, Son of God,
   have mercy on me,
   a sinner.

   b) The Litany of Humility has been attributed to various writers. This version likely comes from St. Margaret Mary. Begin and end each day this week with these words.

   Lord have mercy
   Jesus meek and humble of Heart, listen to my prayers
   From the desire of being esteemed, O Jesus, deliver me.
   From the desire of being known, O Jesus, deliver me.
   From the desire of being praised, O Jesus, deliver me.
   From the desire of being honored, O Jesus, deliver me.
   From the desire of being preferred, O Jesus, deliver me.
   From the desire of being consulted, O Jesus, deliver me.
   From the desire of being approved, O Jesus, deliver me.
   From the desire of being spared, O Jesus, deliver me.
   From the fear of being humbled, O Jesus, deliver me.
   From the fear of being despised, O Jesus, deliver me.
   From the fear of being rebuked, O Jesus, deliver me.

From the fear of being calumniated, O Jesus, deliver me.
From the fear of being forgotten, O Jesus, deliver me.
From the fear of being reviled, O Jesus, deliver me.
From the fear of being ill-treated, O Jesus, deliver me.
From the fear of being injured, O Jesus, deliver me.
O Mary, Mother of the humble, pray for me.
St. Joseph, patron of the humble, pray for me.
St. Michael, who first crushed pride, pray for me.
St. Francis, imitator of a master meek and humble, pray for me.
All you holy spirits sanctified by humility, pray for me.

SESSION FOUR:
VIDEO RESPONSE SHEET

KEY VERSE:
And when they were in the field, Cain rose up against his brother, Abel, and killed him.
(Genesis 4:8b)

Fill in the blanks and take notes as we watch the video together.

1. God's two great gifts to us: _____

2. _____ sees and desires what it _____

   • _____

   • The _____

   • Plain, old

   • Envy is _____

3. But there is _____

> *"But think of the glory of the choice. That makes a man a man. A cat has no choice. A bee must make honey. There's no godliness there. But I have a new love for that glittering instrument, the human soul. It is a lovely and unique thing in the universe.*
>
> *Why, that makes a man great, that gives him stature with the gods, for in his weakness and his filth and his murder of his brother he has still the great choice. He can choose his course and fight it through and win."*
>
> **JOHN STEINBECK EAST OF EDEN**

JOURNAL AND NOTES

SOMETHING OLD, SOMETHING NEW

(Connecting Genesis with the New Testament and the Genius of our Catholic Faith)

"For this is the message, which you have heard from the beginning, that we should love one another, and not be like Cain, who was of the Evil One and murdered his brother. And why did he murder him? Because his own deeds were evil and his brother's righteous. Do not wonder, brethren, that the world hates you. We know that we have passed out of death into life, because we love the brethren. He who does not love remains in death.

Any one who hates his brother is a murderer, and you know that no murderer has eternal life abiding in him. By this, we know love, that he laid down his life for us; and we ought to lay down our lives for the brethren. But if any one has the world's goods and sees his brother in need, yet closes his heart against him, how does God's love abide in him? Little children, let us not love in word or speech but in deed and in truth."

(1 John. 3:11-18)

---

*God gives us free will
so that we can choose to love.*

For Next Time

Please read and complete the Session 5 Study Guide and answer the questions.

At the next session, we will discuss the Study Guide questions and watch the Session 5 Video.

NOTE: Please bring your completed Session 5 Study Guide and your Bible to the next group session.

GOD OF NEW BEGINNINGS

KEY VERSE:
But God remembered Noah and all the
beasts and all the cattle that were with
him in the ark.
(Genesis 8:1a)

05

I. Laying the Foundation

READ: GENESIS 6:5-15; 7:1-5; 8:1, 20-22; 9:1-9, 11-13

You probably learned this story about Noah and the flood when you were a child. But this story is really about God. A steadfast God who refuses to give up on His Creation. A hopeful God who gives rebellious Creation a new beginning.

"The Lord saw that the wickedness of man was great in the earth..." **(6:5)**. God grows angry with humans and their wickedness, but still He remembers Noah. God never forgets His people.

Through Noah, the Lord provides a new beginning for all Creation. Adam and Eve were the first. Now, Noah's family will give human beings a fresh start, a second chance.

Who has not appreciated the chance to make a fresh start?

What's not working in your life? Where are you tired or frustrated? Are you feeling a little bit lost, stuck in a rut with no passion or purpose? What part of your life is not making sense?

We all have needed a fresh start at some point.

Know this: God loves new beginnings.

And you and I love new beginnings too. New Year's Day, the first day on a new job, a first date, or the start of a new semester at school. It is wonderful to have that fresh start and see all the possibilities that lie before you. A chance for life to be different. An opportunity to become a better-version-of-ourselves.

God is always waiting on you:

- just like Jesus waited for the woman at the well, married many times, but always failing
- just like God the Father waited for King David, to help him recover from the horrible mistakes of adultery and murder
- just like the Holy Spirit waited for Mother Teresa to hear a whisper calling her to leave teaching to move to Calcutta to launch something new, and become St. Teresa of Calcutta
- just like the Father waited for the Prodigal Son to come to his right mind and return home to experience a new beginning.

God loves new beginnings, and He is always waiting on us.

How wonderful it is to discover that God never lets go. When our darkest moment arrives, or we have wandered so far away as to think we can never find our way home, God stands ready and offers a new possibility. A second chance. A fresh start.

In many ways, this story of God, Noah, and the flood demonstrate exactly what God is doing in baptism. The waters of baptism wash away our original sin and offer us a new beginning as an adopted child of God. Baptism makes you a part of His family. He will remember you just as he remembered Noah.

Even while we study about Noah, God is at work right now to give you a fresh start.

Rebellious humans, prepare to meet the Lord of new beginnings.

II. This Week's Encounter

GENESIS 6:5-15; 7:1-5; 8:1, 20-22; 9:1-9, 11-13

These passages share the stories of God's displeasure with human disobedience. His heavy heart leads Him to start humankind again. He makes a covenant with Noah to do just that.

Answer the following questions to help you reflect on what you read. **TIP: Circle the questions you find the most interesting or difficult and discuss them with your group at the next session.**

1. **Read Genesis 6:5-8.** Genesis makes it plain. God observes the wickedness. He sees human beings betraying Him. God watches the world continually turn toward evil. Creation resists God. **Verse 6** tells us that it grieves God's heart. So much so that His heart is filled with pain and regret.

    Rebellion, perversion, evil, and corruption abound. In other words, Creation refuses to honor God as God.

    What do you think causes God to have moments of disgust and disappointment today as He surveys the world and how we behave as humans?

    _____

    _____

    _____

    _____

    _____

    _____

2. **Read 6:5-8, 13-15**. God's heart grieves. He is like a troubled parent who suffers at the disobedience and rebellion of His children. Yet, God does not completely abandon His creation. Instead, He decides to preserve a small remnant, starting with Noah and his family. *"But Noah found favor in the eyes of the Lord"* **(6:8)**. Through Noah's family, God will save every species of animal. The Lord is not totally eliminating creation; He is choosing to remake it in a new direction. What seems like destruction instead becomes the Lord's hopeful reconstruction.

Read 1 Kings 19:17-18 and Isaiah 4:2-4

What do you notice in these two passages?

What do these verses say about God?

----

3. **Read 7:1-5**. Notice Noah's remarkable obedience.

   In 6:8, "Noah found favor in the eyes of the Lord."

   6:22 emphasizes Noah's faithfulness and obedience.

   What other characteristics of Noah might have found favor with God?

   _____

   _____

   _____

   _____

   _____

   How do you think Noah felt when he realized that God planned to destroy nearly all of Creation and all of his fellow human beings?

   _____

   _____

   _____

   _____

   _____

   How might Noah have felt when God selected him to be the new beginning?

   _____

   _____

   _____

   _____

Imagine what it was like to construct a huge ark and make plans while all the people around you either rejected God or did not believe the plan.

Can you think of a few saints who sincerely tried to follow God when everyone around them did not understand them or even rejected them?

_____

_____

_____

_____

_____

Have you ever paid a price for trying to obey God in your own life?

_____

_____

_____

_____

_____

4. **Read 8:1, 6-13, 20-22**. Notice how God's heart is comforted and turns.

   In **8:1**, God "remembered Noah." This moment provides the dramatic turning point of the story.

   Compare that to
   - **Genesis 19:29**
   - **Genesis 30:22**
   - **Exodus 2:24**

What do these passages teach us about God?

_____

_____

_____

_____

_____

_____

In **8:20-22**, observe how Noah's first act is to build an altar and worship God. In turn, God's heart shifts into a new promise and new relationship with His people.

What do these verses say about God's heart?

_____

_____

_____

_____

_____

_____

5. Read **9:1, 3-9, 11-13**. (and remember **6:18**). The story has now moved from judgment to new creation. God does not give up on His creation or on the possibilities for human beings. Chaos and evil do not have the final word. God creates a new beginning. And makes a bold promise.

Notice how God reinstates man and gives him a job to do much like He did with Adam and Eve: be fruitful, multiply. And notice how the idea of being made in the image of God plays an important role again here.

God establishes a new covenant. This crucial moment with Noah lays the foundation for the covenant God will make with Abraham in the next session.

Describe the covenant promise God makes here with Noah.

Finally, notice how God places the bow in the sky as a reminder of that covenant. Ancient warriors hung up their bows as a sign of their retirement from battle. In this image here, God promises never to take aim at the whole earth and its people again.

6. Our key verse is

> "But **God remembered** Noah and all the beasts and all the cattle
> that were with him in the ark."
> **(Genesis 8:1a)**

These are life-changing words. God remembers. He doesn't forget or abandon His chosen people. God never lets go. Even in the darkest times of disobedience and rebellion, He still provides a future.

Have you seen God at work in this way in the world, in your parish, or in your own life?

----

7. **Noah is a man of great virtue.** Just as the previous session taught us that life is choices, Noah reinforces that lesson. When we use our free will for God, humans have capacity for great good. Like Noah, we can become co-laborers with the One who made us.

6:8	Noah found favor in the sight of the Lord
6:9	Noah was a righteous man, blameless in his generation
6:9	Noah walked with God
6:22	Noah did all that God commanded him
7:5	Noah did all that the Lord had commanded him
9:1	God blessed Noah and his sons and said to them, "Be fruitful and multiply, and fill the earth."

After reading his story, what are three words you would use to describe Noah?

----

8. Take a look at **John 8:2-11**. In this powerful story, Jesus demonstrates how our Lord is a God of new beginnings. Compare what the crowd says in **8:4** to what Jesus tells the woman caught in adultery in verse **8:11**.

III. Just for You: Experiencing God

This section will not be discussed in the group setting. It is designed specifically to help grow your own personal relationship with God.

1. God's heart delights at new beginnings. Even when we feel far away, still God is at work to do a new thing in our lives.

    Think about the areas of your life: your family, relationships, work, emotional well-being, financial stability, spiritual life, hobbies, and so on.

    Are there areas in your life that feel beyond help? A relationship broken beyond repair? A loved one who has wandered from the family and not likely to return? An addiction that is crippling you or someone you love?

    _____

    _____

    _____

    _____

    _____

    _____

    _____

    _____

    _____

    Invite the God of new beginnings to help you envision the impossible becoming possible. The impossible becoming real.

2. Take a moment this week to remember your baptism and the big promises God makes to you.

Because of your baptism, God promises to:

- Forgive all your sins
- Adopt you into His own family
- Make you a "new creature" and a "partaker of the divine nature"
- Build you into a temple of the Holy Spirit
(CCC1265-1267)

Stop by a parish this week, and make the sign of the cross on your forehead with the holy water there. Give thanks to God for your baptism. Thank Him for making you His own. You are a baptized child of God. His covenant promises are bold....and true.

You are somebody. You are a child of God. Use these words to remind yourself of who you are.

———————

I am the child of a great King.
He is my Father and my God.
The world may praise me or criticize me.
It matters not.
He is with me,
Always at my side,
Guiding and protecting me.
I do not fear
Because
I AM HIS.

SESSION FIVE:
VIDEO RESPONSE SHEET

KEY VERSE:
But God remembered Noah and all the beasts and all the cattle that were with him in the ark.
(Genesis 8:1a)

Fill in the blanks and take notes as we watch the video together.

1. God's Bold Promise: _____

2. Obstacles _____

   • Lack of _____

   • _____

   • Fear of _____

   • Need to _____

3. It only takes 1 thing: _____

   • To see _____

   • To _____

JOURNAL AND NOTES

SOMETHING OLD, SOMETHING NEW

(Connecting Genesis with the New Testament and the Genius of our Catholic Faith)

"For in Christ Jesus you are all sons of God, through faith.
For as many of you as were baptized into Christ have put on Christ."

(Galatians 3:26-27)

———

Baptism is the ultimate new beginning.

———

For Next Time

Please read and complete the Session 6 Study Guide and answer the questions.

At the next session, we will discuss the Study Guide questions and watch the Session 6 Video.

NOTE: Please bring your completed Session 6 Study Guide and your Bible to the next group session.

GOD'S BOLD PROMISES

KEY VERSE:
Now the Lord said to Abram, "Go....to
the land that I will show you...And I will
make of you a great nation."
(Gen. 12:1-2)

06

I. Laying the Foundation

READ: GENESIS 12:1-8, 15:1-6, 17:1-22

Abraham is a hero of the faith. In fact, his story becomes the defining story of Genesis.

God makes a bold choice. He has created the world, grieved human wickedness, and re-booted the world through Noah and his family. But the Lord still finds frustration in the rebellious decisions of His children. So God chooses His own special people.

God makes a bold promise. The story of God's special people will begin with Abraham. Through Abraham, God will begin His unique relationship with the people of Israel. Abraham will start it all.

When we meet Abraham, he is not a likely candidate for what God promises to do. Abraham, seventy-five years old, and his wife, Sarah, have been unable to have children. Nevertheless, the Lord invites Abraham to believe in the promise of a bold, new future. Life in a new place. Life with a child who will be Abraham's first descendant and the firstborn of what will become God's chosen people, Israel.

It doesn't matter what your past looks like. With God, the future is always bigger than your past. Abraham's story is an invitation to open yourself up to the incredible things God has in store for you next. Maybe God is calling you to start over, take a risk, do something completely different, or embrace what is before you with renewed passion. Just know this: when you make yourself available to God, He will lead and love you more than you have ever imagined. He not only makes bold promises; He keeps them.

Now is your time. Your God-given destiny awaits you. Just like He did with Abraham, God wants to draw us out of our own little worlds to give us a bigger vision of ourselves, a bigger vision of God, and a bigger vision of what is possible.

So, with all that we know about the past, we are invited to step bravely into the future, an uncertain future. Our faith gives us the courage to step boldly into the uncertain future hoping for good things.

The Lord simply tells Abraham to "go." Remarkably, like Noah, Abraham responds with obedience. He "goes" just as the Lord asks.

God makes big promises not only to Abraham but to all his descendants. And because of his faith, Abraham cooperates with God to settle Canaan, the Promised Land.

Genesis pieces the story of Abraham together masterfully. This drama sets up the essential element of the Old Testament: God's special bond with His people Israel. Here's how the story unfolds:

Genesis 12: God makes bold promises to Abraham
    Genesis 15: God makes His covenant with Abraham
        Genesis 16: Abraham and Sarah fail to trust God's promises
            Genesis 17-18: God makes the promises once again
                Genesis 21: Sarah gives birth to the long awaited son, Isaac
                  Genesis 22: God tests Abraham's faith

In Abraham's story, we experience God's powerful promises. We encounter Abraham's powerful response: Faith. Abraham's covenant becomes ours through Jesus Christ. No story is more important. Because of faith, we are all related to Abraham.

It is hard to believe. But it all begins right here with an elderly couple named Abraham and Sarah. Abraham: a man who chooses to believe God's bold promises and then takes action. His faith gives birth to the covenant that has changed our lives.

Abraham and Sarah, prepare to meet God, the ultimate Promise-Keeper.

II. *This Week's Encounter*

GENESIS 12:1-8, 15:1-6, 17:1-22

These passages convey crucial foundations of our faith: Abraham's courageous faith; his trust in God's promises; his obedience; and God's bold promise to create a special bond, a covenant, with His chosen people, Israel.

Answer the following questions to help you digest what you read. **TIP: Circle the questions you find most interesting or difficult and discuss them with your group at the next session.**

1. **Read Genesis 12:1**: *Now the Lord said to Abram, "Go from your country and your kindred and your father's house to the Land that I will show you."*

    Imagine what it was like to be Abraham, a 75-year old man with no children, living a stable, settled life with your kinfolk. God calls you and invites you to leave behind your land, your extended family, and your entire past. It is as if everything up until now in your life is irrelevant. Most challenging of all, God does not even tell you where you will be going. The Lord simply says He will eventually show you the desired place when you get there. How would you describe the feelings Abraham likely experienced?

    _____

    _____

    _____

    _____

    _____

2. **Read Genesis 12:2-3**. God makes bold promises to Abraham. Underline these promises in your own Bible and reflect on what Abraham must have thought of these powerful words from God.

   a)   *I will make of you a great nation*

   b)   *I will bless you*

   c)   *I will make your name great*

   d)   *You will be a blessing*

   e)   *I will bless those who bless you and curse those who curse you*

   f)   *By you, all the families of the earth shall bless themselves*

3. **Read Genesis 15:1-6**, **18-21**. Abraham and Sarah have now traveled and followed God for some time. But they still have not yet received the child or the land that God promised them in **Genesis 12**.

   As Abraham speaks with God, notice the pattern of conversation:
   God promises,
        Abraham resists and desires a sign of reassurance,
   God reaffirms the promise again,
        and then Abraham finally accepts it.

   a)   **GOD:** *Do not be afraid, Abram, I am your shield; your reward shall be very great*

   Do not be afraid. This is one of God's favorite things to tell us human beings when we fear, doubt, or resist. Take a quick look at these verses and write down who the Lord is addressing in each of these instances.

   Gen. 26:24   Gen. 46:3   Deut. 1:21   Isa. 41:10   Luke 1:30-31

b)   **ABRAHAM:** *O Lord, God, what will you give me, for I continue childless...?*

c)   **GOD:** *Look toward heaven and number the stars...So shall your descendants be*

d)   **ABRAHAM:** *And he believed the Lord; and God reckoned it to him as righteousness*

God promises. Abraham believes. Abraham trusts God. As a result, Abraham becomes the model for us all. God gives Abraham full title to His promises and their fulfillment. Faith and trust. That's what God calls us to.

What do they say about faith and what it means to fully trust God?

_____

_____

_____

_____

_____

How do these verses speak to you?

_____

_____

_____

_____

_____

e)   **Look at Genesis 15:18**. God makes a covenant. This is the land that will belong to Abraham and his descendants. It is God's promise.

4.   **Read 17:1-22. God doubles down on the covenant and His promises.**

Abraham is now 99 years old. Surely, by this time, Abraham and Sarah's faith must be wearing thin. They have been waiting for the complete fulfillment of God's promises for almost 25 years.

Have you ever waited for a long time for God to answer a prayer? If so, describe what that felt like and anything that it caused you to do or not do.

In these verses, it is almost like God is asking for even more faith and trust from Abraham before all the promises are fulfilled. God is preparing Abraham: with a new name, with circumcision, and with a name change for Sarah as well.

First, notice the name change in **17:5**. 'Abram' becomes 'Abraham." God is reinforcing His promises in a very special way. He changes Abram (which means 'exalted ancestor') to Abraham (which means 'ancestor of a multitude'). In other words, Abraham has a bold, new name before he even has the child the name promises.

Then, notice in **17:9-14** that God next instructs Abraham to circumcise himself and all the male descendants who follow him afterward. This circumcision will be a sign of the people's covenant with God. Again, God asks for the circumcision before Abraham even has the child that the circumcision promises.

In **17:15-16 and 17:19**, notice how the promise is specifically made to Sarah, and her name is changed too (meaning "princess). This promise comes after Sarah's patience has run out and she tries to fulfill God's promise of a child through another woman (Hagar) in **Genesis 16**. God explicitly promises to her the gift of Isaac.

Finally, in **17:17**, notice Abraham's reaction to God's promise that Sarah will give birth at age 90. He laughs. Soon after, Sarah will laugh at the same news in **18:11-14**. Interestingly, the child's name "Isaac" is a play on the Hebrew word for "laugh."

Like Mary will eventually receive from the angel Gabriel, Sarah here receives startling news. She will bear a child. And it will be a miracle. God does indeed make bold promises. And He delivers.

If you were Abraham and Sarah at this point, do you think you would have still been willing to trust God's promises of a son and new land for your descendants? Would you have had questions like they did? Do you think you would have laughed?

----

5. In many ways, this story of Abraham and Sarah defines the Christian faith.

   Like God did with them, He makes promises in a covenant with us. This happens in our baptism. There, God forgives our sins. He promises to love and nourish us always. He makes us a part of His family. Through baptism, we belong to Him.

   God makes many promises to us. In fact, just like He did with Sarah and Abraham, God can even bring new life where there appears to be no possibility for it at all. The Lord, the Giver of Life, can even bring new life to the dead. Time and again, we are reminded that we are Easter people.

   How does the story of Abraham and Sarah help you? Inspire you?

III. Just for You: Experiencing God

This section will not be discussed in the group setting. It is designed specifically to help grow your own personal relationship with God.

1. How do you seek to hear the voice of God in your own life?
   - As you read Genesis?
   - As you discuss with a group of fellow believers?
   - As you pray in the classroom of silence?

How might the Lord intervene and help you?

----

2. The Sacraments help us experience the promises of God. In many ways, the Sacraments pour out the power of God's covenant into your life.

At Baptism, you are made a part of God's family, the Church.

In Reconciliation, you can experience God's promise to forgive and heal you.

At Mass, you can receive the precious body and blood of Jesus, who welcomes you and nourishes your soul.

In Marriage, the covenant bond between husband and wife is expressed in the same way that God's love is shared with the Church.

How faithful are you to experience the sacraments regularly?

----

3. Spending some time in adoration of the Blessed Sacrament can provide the opportunity to reflect on life's big questions. Being alone with Christ Jesus in the classroom of silence can help you tune your ears to hear God's voice in your life.

Today is a great day to schedule your next time for adoration. Find out when your parish offers this opportunity and put a reminder on your calendar.

When you go to adoration, remember Abraham and Sarah. They obeyed God, walked with God, found favor with God, and seized the opportunity to be a part of God's bold promises. You can experience that too!

VIDEO RESPONSE SHEET

12 Very Bold Promises Of God

WE SAY:	GOD SAYS:
It's impossible	All things are possible **(Luke 18:27)**
I'm too tired	I will give you rest **(Matthew 11:28-30)**
Nobody loves me	I love you **(John 3:16)**
I can't figure things out	I direct your steps **(Proverbs 20:24)**
I can't do it	You can do all things **(Philippians 4:13)**
I'm not able	I am able to provide you with every blessing in abundance **(2 Cor. 9:8)**
It's not worth it	It will be worth it **(Rom 8.28)**
I just can't forgive myself	I forgive you **(1 John 1:9)**
I can't manage	I will supply all your needs **(Philippians 4:12)**
I'm afraid	Be not afraid **(Luke 1:30)**
I'm always worried and frustrated	Cast your anxieties on me **(1Peter 5:7)**
I feel so alone	I will never leave you nor forsake you **(Hebrews 13:5)**

JOURNAL AND NOTES

SOMETHING OLD, SOMETHING NEW

(Connecting Genesis with the New Testament and the Genius of our Catholic Faith)

And Mary said, "Behold, I am the handmaid of the Lord; let it be to me according to your word."

(Luke 1:38)

Sarah's "Yes" made her the mother of nations.

Mary's "Yes" made her the Mother of God.

For Next Time

Please read and complete the Session 7 Study Guide and answer the questions.

At the next session, we will discuss the Study Guide questions and watch the Session 7 Video.

NOTE: Please bring your completed Session 7 Study Guide and your Bible to the next group session.

SAY YES

KEY VERSE:
So Abram went, as the Lord had told him...Abram was 75 years old when he departed Haran.
(Genesis 12:4)

07

I. Laying the Foundation
READ: GENESIS 12:1-20, 16:1-6, 18:1-15

Abraham and Sarah are far from perfect people. Evidently, you can be heroes of the faith and still have your flaws. God often writes straight with crooked lines.

At times, Abraham and Sarah are skeptical of God and His promises. In a crisis, Abraham lies and acts like a coward. After waiting for years for the child God has promised, Sarah takes matters into her own hands rather than trusting God. She tries to work around the situation when she thinks God is not delivering on His promise.

Nearly 25 years after leaving his homeland to embrace God's promises, Abraham laughs at the notion that he will become a father at age 100. Sarah laughs at that same promise as well. And the heavenly messengers respond, "Is anything too wonderful for the Lord?" You and I know the answer to that.

Turn to God making yourself available and He will cast aside your guilt, your shame, and all the doubts you have about yourself. You can place your hope in the certainty that for thousands of years God has been using men and women of all ages to do incredible things. Now it is your turn.

Like most of us, Abraham and Sarah's faith journey is filled with twists and turns, doubts and fears. But, remarkably, almost miraculously, they persist and cling to God's promises for nearly twenty-five years. They wait on God, albeit imperfectly, trusting Him to deliver on the promise of a child, a first descendant. As a result, Sarah, aged 90, finally gives birth to Isaac.

God makes good on His promise to establish Abraham's descendants as a special people. And He does so because Abraham and Sarah say "Yes." They believe God's promises. They partner with God and cooperate with His plan to fulfill His purpose. Quite simply, they trust the Lord.

Abraham says Yes to leave his entire life behind to go where God leads. Sarah says Yes to being the bearer of the promised child, Isaac. She gives us a first inkling of Mary, who will come and say "Yes" to bearing Jesus, the Christ.

Christians should be the ultimate people of possibility. But too often we are people of impossibility, people of "No" rather than people of "Yes." Suggest that something new or different be done in your community and often all you will hear are reasons why it cannot be done. "We don't have enough money." "It won't work." "We've already tried something like that before."

God is more interested in your future than He is in your past – but He is perhaps most interested in your now. What would your life look like if you gave Him your deepest "Yes"? If you chose to hold nothing back. If you wholeheartedly began intentionally living to become the best version of yourself today. Not only what would your life look like but what would the world begin to look like if each of us offered a complete Yes to the Lord.

Faith and trust. Even when life is no garden party. Even when the wait is long. Because of his faith, Abraham discovered that nothing is impossible for our Lord.

Abraham is the father of our faith. His faith defines our faith.

Skeptical world, prepare to meet the God for whom all things are possible.

II. This Week's Encounter

GENESIS 12:1-20, 16:1-6, 18:1-15

These passages convey Abraham's courageous faith. His obedience, even his shortcomings and disappointments. In the end, Abraham and Sarah discover the miraculous power of God.

Answer the following questions to help you digest what you read. **TIP: Circle the questions you find most interesting or difficult and discuss them with your group at the next session.**

1. **Read Genesis 12:1**: *Now the Lord said to Abram, "Go from your country and your kindred and your father's house to the Land that I will show you."*

    Read Genesis 12:4. *"So Abram went as the Lord had told him."*

    When God invites, Abraham acts. Immediately. He does so unquestioningly. He trusts the Lord and obeys Him completely. This 75-year old man makes a radical decision of obedience to do exactly what God tells him to do.

    Look at Mark 1:16-20. Compare the decision there by Simon, Andrew, James and John to Abraham's decision here. How are they similar? How do they differ?

    ----

2. **Read Genesis 12:10-20**. Abraham's faith is remarkable. But it is not perfect. In his faith journey, he displays great strength like he does in **12:1-9**, boldly leaving everything behind to go into God's future. But he also displays weakness. In fact, as you carefully read Abraham's journey from **Genesis 12-25**, you will discover that his sincere acts of faith are often quickly followed by moments of failure.

   In this passage, fear causes him to lose courage and the faith to trust God. Abraham falls into dishonesty. It quickly becomes clear that this journey will depend on God's direction and protection rather than on Abraham's strength or smarts.

   Can you remember a time in your own life when you depended more on yourself than you did on God?

   ----

3. **Read Genesis 16:1-16**. Sarah goes along with Abraham every step of the way. She doesn't abandon him even though many people around them must have thought Abraham had lost his mind to trust God enough to go to an unknown land and become a father at such a late age.

   But, after more than a decade of waiting for a child to arrive, Sarah sure must be questioning God at this point. She doubts whether she will have that promised child. So Sarah takes matters into her own hands. She seizes the initiative, and Abraham weakly agrees to conceive a child through Sarah's maid, Hagar.

In a way, Sarah is heroic, since it was perfectly legal for a man to do this with the permission of his barren wife. Sarah thinks she is solving the problem. Really, however, she is allowing her fears and doubts to take control. And creating more problems than solutions.

What is one important moment in your life when you have doubted God in a deep way?

What was the experience of doubting God like? Did it ultimately make you trust Him more or less?

----

4. **Read Genesis 18:1-15**. Notice how this story captures Abraham at his best: warm, generous, and welcoming. His kindness to strangers sets the stage for a powerful encounter with messengers from the Lord.

In **v. 10**, these messengers give a great gift in return: God's birth announcement to Sarah. Like Abraham in **Genesis 17**, Sarah finds this laughable. After all, she is in her nineties. But the heavenly messengers respond, "Is anything too wonderful for the Lord?"

As we will soon see in the next session about **Genesis 21**, God intends to have the last laugh.

Consider how often welcoming hospitality and kindness to strangers are emphasized in the Scriptures.

Read Matthew 25:31-46. Notice how Jesus emphasizes that hospitality and generosity mark the difference between heaven and hell.

Read Luke 10:25-37. Jesus again demonstrates how hospitality and generosity have eternal consequences.

Have you ever felt really close to God after welcoming someone you did not know or after being exceedingly generous to someone in need?

----

5. Abraham and Sarah are not perfect. Not even close. Abraham doesn't always trust God. Their doubts bring trouble and suffering. In other words, Abraham and Sarah are a lot like us.

Yet, by faith, their lives are transformed. They enter a new land. They welcome a new son. They launch a new future together with God. And their faith becomes the bedrock for the promises Christ makes to you and me.

Why? Because they said "Yes" and made themselves available to the Lord.

God remains faithful. He invites us to trust Him completely.

Believing brings passion and purpose. It doesn't leave us stuck in our missteps. Faith bears fruit. And then it leads to joy.

Have you ever said a deep "Yes" to God?

----

6. **Read Romans 4 below.** Notice how St. Paul makes Abraham's faith the model for our faith as Christians. The story of Genesis becomes a critical part of our faith and it is nowhere made more plain than in these important verses.

    *... It depends on faith, in order that **the promise may rest on grace and be guaranteed to all his descendants—... to those who share the faith of Abraham, for he is the father of us all**, as it is written, "I have made you the father of many nations"—in the presence of the God in whom he believed, who gives life to the dead and calls into existence the things that do not exist.*

In hope he believed against hope, that he should become the father of many nations; as he had been told, "So shall your descendants be." He did not weaken in faith when he considered his own body, which was as good as dead because he was about a hundred years old, or when he considered the barrenness of Sarah's womb. No distrust made him waver concerning the promise of God, but he grew strong in his faith as he gave glory to God, fully convinced that God was able to do what he had promised

*... **But the words, "it was reckoned to him," were written not for his sake alone, but for ours also. It will be reckoned to us who believe in him that raised from the dead Jesus our Lord, who was put to death for our trespasses and raised for our justification.***

What is one thing these verses teach you about your own faith?

III. Just for You: Experiencing God

This section will not be discussed in the group setting. It is designed specifically to help grow your own personal relationship with God.

1. In their own way, Abraham and Sarah each said "Yes" to God. The Lord invited them out of their comfort zone. God's bold promises are not merely for us to be comfortable or to remain in the status quo. He invites us to bold transformation. To allow Him to transform us fully into the best-version-of-ourselves.

    So Abraham and Sarah said "Yes." They made themselves available. That's how it begins: by making ourselves truly available to God. Imperfectly to be sure. But available nonetheless.

    Abraham and Sarah did not turn back. They pushed forward to become who God wanted them to be. They knew He had something greater in mind for them than they could ever imagine for themselves.

    So they said Yes.

    Have you ever said Yes? A complete "Yes" to the Lord? Have there been multiple times in your life when you gave God your deepest Yes?

If so, describe some of your experience? Do you remember a particular moment when "the light went on" for you? Or was it more like slowly opening window shades and allowing the light to gradually fill the room?

You will be amazed at what happens when we make ourselves completely available to God. What might God have in mind for you?

List a few dreams you believe God has given you that you have never pursued.

List a few words you believe God would use to describe you at your best.

_____

_____

_____

_____

_____

2. Allow Abraham and Sarah to inspire you. Invite God to do in you more than you could imagine ever being done. Make yourself available. An excellent way to begin is to pray this prayer of transformation.

Lord,
Here I am.
I trust that you have an incredible plan for me.
Today I surrender my whole being to your care.
I surrender my life, my plans, and my very self to you.
I make myself 100 percent available to you today.
Transform me. Transform my life.
Everything is on the table.
Take what you want to take,
and give what you want to give.
Transform me into the person you created me to be,
so I can live the life you envisioned for me at the beginning of time.
I hold nothing back.
I am 100 percent available.
Lead me, challenge me, encourage me,
and open my eyes to all your amazing possibilities.
Show me what it is you want me to do, and I will do it.
Amen.

SESSION SEVEN:
VIDEO RESPONSE SHEET

KEY VERSE:

So Abram went, as the Lord had told him...Abram was 75 years old when he departed Haran.
(Genesis 12:4)

Fill in the blanks and take notes as we watch the video together.

1. The Enemies of 'Yes':
   a) _____
   b) _____
   c) _____
   d) _____

2. _____: A New Way of _____

We walk by faith not by sight
(2 Corinthians 5:7)

JOURNAL AND NOTES

SOMETHING OLD, SOMETHING NEW

(Connecting Genesis with the New Testament and the Genius of our Catholic Faith)

By faith Abraham obeyed when he was called to go out to a place which he was to receive as an inheritance; and he went out, not knowing where he was to go.

By faith he sojourned in the land of promise, as in a foreign land, living in tents with Isaac and Jacob, heirs with him of the same promise. For he looked forward to the city which has foundations, whose builder and maker is God.

By faith Sarah herself received power to conceive, even when she was past the age, since she considered him faithful who had promised.

Therefore, from one man, and him as good as dead, were born descendants as many as the stars of heaven and as the innumerable grains of sand by the seashore.

(Hebrews 11:8-12)

With their faith,

Abraham and Sarah began God's family.

With your faith, you too can enjoy a future

that is bigger than your past.

For Next Time

Please read and complete the Session 8 Study Guide and answer the questions.

At the next session, we will discuss the Study Guide questions and watch the Session 8 Video.

NOTE: Please bring your completed Session 8 Study Guide and your Bible to the next group session.

ONLY GOD!

KEY VERSE:
"...because you have done this, and have not withheld your son, your only-begotten son, I will indeed bless you, and I will multiply your descendants as the stars of heaven and as the sand which is on the seashore..."
(Gen. 22:16-17)

08

I. Laying the Foundation

READ: GENESIS 21:1-8, 22:1-18

When it comes to faith and obedience, Father Abraham is unmatched. In fact, his faith story still echoes across the world even today. For more than 3000 years, the names of Abraham and Sarah have been known in every generation.

Remember again the flow of the full story:

Genesis 12: God makes bold promises to Abraham

  Genesis 15: God makes His covenant with Abraham

    Genesis 16: Abraham and Sarah fail to trust God's promises

      Genesis 18: God makes the promise of a son once again

        Genesis 21: Sarah gives birth to the long awaited son, Isaac

        Genesis 22: God tests Abraham's faith

As we reach **Genesis 21**, Sarah takes center stage. The promised child arrives. Sarah gives birth to Isaac. After decades of waiting on God to fulfill His promise, He does just that. You can almost feel the tears of joy flowing down Sarah's cheeks and the wonder in Abraham's heart as they welcome and hold the little boy.

Then Abraham moves front and center in **Genesis 22**. God tests Abraham in one of the most powerful scenes of the entire Bible. After all these years of clinging to God's promises, Abraham is asked to sacrifice his beloved son to God.

Tension drips from the page as we read this story. Abraham, the loving father, does his best to obey God's striking command to kill Isaac in sacrifice to the One who provided the boy in the first place. Genesis does not tell us why God chooses to test Abraham. Somehow, even after all that Abraham and Sarah have endured, God says Abraham must surrender his beloved son.

Sometimes the cost of being a disciple is high. When you sincerely try to live the Gospel and embrace the Catholic faith, you will encounter tests. No question about it. Grace is free, but it is not cheap.

Somehow, Abraham saw his way through. Somehow he walked by faith not by sight. Somehow he knew that God is at work in our lives, even when we think He is not. God is in control, even when it appears that everything is falling apart. God has a different way of doing things – a better way.

How do you see your way through a test of your faith? How do you find spiritual water when your soul is parched? Do the next right thing. The surest way to find life is to do what you know to be the next right thing, right now. If you do the next right thing often enough for long enough, you will live your way into the incredible life God has designed just for you.

Remarkably, Abraham's obedience here is greater than at any other time in his entire life. Somehow, Abraham discovers again that faith in God alone is the path to a good life. That we have been made by God, for God.

In the end, Abraham passes the test. This has been a test. Only a test. And Abraham holds nothing back. His obedience is complete and unquestioned. And God reaffirms the very same promises He made to Abraham all the way back in **Genesis 12:1-3**. Abraham's descendants, beginning with Isaac himself, shall be numerous and great. They shall be God's very own people.

Abraham has again proven himself to be the father of faith. We are his children and descendants.

World, prepare to meet the Lord, the God of Abraham, Sarah, and, now, Isaac.

II. This Week's Encounter

GENESIS 21:1-8, 22:1-18

These passages convey a whole new level of faith and obedience. God tests Abraham. Somehow Abraham passes the test. And God's reaffirms His bold promises to create a special bond with His chosen people, Israel.

Answer the following questions to help you digest what you read. **TIP: Circle the questions you find most interesting or difficult and discuss them with your group at the next session.**

1. **Read Genesis 21:1-8**: At last! The promised child arrives! Sarah gives birth. Abraham is about 100 years old at this point. Remember this is 25 years after God made the initial promise of a child to Abraham back in **Genesis 12**.

   God is faithful. He keeps His promise. The Lord may arrive later than expected, but He never arrives too late.

   Finally, Sarah and Abraham have the long-awaited child, Isaac. This son is the first descendant of Abraham. God makes good on His promise just as Abraham had believed and obeyed. This is the nature of a covenant, God's makes promises and we respond in faith to receive.

   St. Ignatius of Loyola liked to read Scripture and meditate on it by imagining himself as being present in the story. He would envision himself as different persons in the story and as a spectator in various locations of the story. He would then try to experience the sights, smells, sounds, thoughts and feelings in each person or setting. Place yourself in this story at the birth of Isaac, either as one of the characters or as a spectator watching the events unfold.

Describe the scene, the smells and the sounds. What are some of the emotions and feelings that are being experienced?

_____

_____

_____

_____

How might Sarah have reacted to seeing and holding Isaac? This little baby represented so many hopes and dreams. Think how she must have remembered all the suffering and endurance and faith that has preceded this moment.

_____

_____

_____

_____

2. Sarah rejoices in the birth and her new station in life: mother. The child is obediently named Isaac, which means "God laughed." Remember how Sarah and Abraham both laughed at the idea of God giving them a child when they were at such a late age. But God is faithful. The Lord has the last laugh, and He shares it with Sarah in **verse 6**!

We can understand Sarah's doubts over the years. However, the name of Isaac serves as a reminder that there is no need for doubt when it comes to God and His promises.

What is one time in your life when you have waited on God? Or a time when you searched for God's presence in your life but were unable to find it?

What was that experience of waiting on God, or searching for Him, like? Did it make you trust Him more or less?

3. As you read **Genesis 21:1-8**, what do these verses tell you about Abraham?

About God?

-----

4. **Read Genesis 22: 1-14**. Notice how the suspense builds every step of the way. These verses are so powerful and gut-wrenching. Again, like St. Ignatius would, envision yourself at different places or as different people in this story.

What do you notice most of all? What are you feeling?

What do you think Isaac was expecting?

Did Sarah know about what was happening?

How excruciating must have been the pain in Abraham's heart?

5. **Notice verses 1, 7-8, and 11-12.**

   What do these verses tell us about Abraham?

About God?

_____

_____

_____

_____

_____

_____

Can you recall a time when you believe you were being tested? What was that experience like?

_____

_____

_____

_____

_____

_____

What have you learned from that experience?

_____

_____

_____

_____

_____

_____

6. Again, in many ways, the story of Abraham defines the Christian faith. In this remarkable story, God asks Abraham to sacrifice his long-awaited son, Isaac. Abraham must have struggled internally in a mighty way, but he begins to act in full obedience to God. When God sees that faithful trust, He stops Abraham's sacrifice. In the end, the sacrifice is not required. Only faith. And complete trust.

Only God would sacrifice His only begotten Son to save us. He does for us what He would never ask us to do ourselves. In fact, we cannot do it for ourselves. The Lord makes the sacrifice to set us right with Him. He does it for us. It is a gift. A gift of love. And we receive it in faith.

How does the story of Abraham help you? Inspire you?

III. *Just for You: Experiencing God*

This section will not be discussed in the group setting. It is designed specifically to help grow your own personal relationship with God.

1. God will remain faithful. He keeps His promises.

    Here are five wonderful promises God makes to you. In a way, they represent the dreams He has in mind for you.

I love you

(John 3:16)

I will never leave you nor forsake you

Keep your lives free from the love of money, and be content with what you have because God has said, "Never will I leave you; never will I forsake you."

(Heb. 13.5)

I give you strength over temptation

Finally, be strong in the Lord and in His mighty power. Put on the full armor of God so that you can take your stand against the devil's schemes.

(Eph. 6.10-11)

I give you abundant life, now

I have come that they may have life, and have it to the full.

(John 10.10)

I go to prepare a place for you

Do not let your hearts be troubled. Trust in God; trust also in me. In my Father's house are many rooms; if it were not so, I would have told you. I am going there to prepare a place for you.

(John 14.1-3)

Which of these promises speaks most to you right now? Why?

---

2. How can you respond with faith to the promises of God in your life?

Prayer is one excellent step to begin building your faith and trust in God. Here are two suggestions for ways to grow forward one step in prayer:

- Pray the Prayer of Transformation from page 116 each day this week to begin your day

- For the next seven days, use the Dynamic Catholic Prayer Process on the next page to begin to create a daily habit of having a conversation with God

The Dynamic Catholic Prayer Process

Here is the basic prayer process that our team at Dynamic Catholic uses and suggests as a starting point for building your own prayer relationship with God. We developed this simple process after studying hundreds of prayer styles and disciplines from many Catholic spiritualities. Again, the point is forming a simple, regular habit, five to ten minutes a day. Daily prayer IS your relationship with God.

1. **Gratitude** – Begin by thanking God in a personal dialogue for whatever you are most grateful for today.

2. **Awareness** – Revisit the times in the past twenty-four hours when you were and were not the-best-version-of-yourself. Talk to God about these situations and ask Him to give you the gift of greater awareness when similar situations arise in the future.

3. **Significant Moments** – Identify something you experienced today and explore what God might be trying to say to you through that event.

4. **Peace** – Ask God to forgive you for any wrong you have committed (against yourself, another person, or him) and fill you with a deep and abiding peace.

5. **Freedom** – Talk to God about how He is inviting you to change your life so you can experience the freedom that comes from knowing that who you are, where you are, and what you are doing makes sense. Is He inviting you to rethink the way you do things? Is God asking you to let go of something or someone? Is He asking you to hold on to something or someone?

6. **Pray for Others** - Pray for those you feel called to pray for today, and those who have asked you to pray for them recently. Take a moment and pray for these people by name, asking God to bless and guide them.

Finish by praying the Our Father

VIDEO RESPONSE SHEET

KEY VERSE:

"…because you have done this, and have not withheld your son, your only-begotten son, I will indeed bless you, and I will multiply your descendants as the stars of heaven and as the sand which is on the seashore…" (Gen. 22:16-17)

Fill in the blanks and take notes as we watch the video together.

1. _____: What's _____

2. _____ verse in the Bible?

    After these things, God tested Abraham

3. What are you afraid of?
    a) Fear of the _____
    b) Fear of _____
    c) Fear of _____
    d) Fear of the _____

4. _____ Is Always _____

    _____ verse in the Bible = *The Lord will provide*

JOURNAL AND NOTES

SOMETHING OLD, SOMETHING NEW

(Connecting Genesis with the New Testament and the Genius of our Catholic Faith)

While we were yet helpless, at the right time Christ died for the ungodly.

Why, one will hardly die for a righteous man—though perhaps for a good man one will dare even to die.

But God shows his love for us in that while we were yet sinners Christ died for us.

(Romans 5:6-8)

———————

Only God would sacrifice

His only begotten Son to save us.

He does for us what we cannot do for ourselves.

The Lord makes the sacrifice

to set us right with Him.

He does it for us. It is a gift.

A gift of love. And we receive it in faith.

———————

MOVING FORWARD

Congratulations! You've read lots of Genesis and discovered the crucial stories that teach us who we really are.

How has this experience shaped your own journey and experience of the Lord?

_____

_____

_____

_____

_____

_____

_____

What is one excellent next step you can take to deepen your faith and love for God? What's the next right thing to do? How can you make this next step a reality?

_____

_____

_____

_____

_____

_____

_____

This eight-week journey has helped you experience the grace of God at work in your life. What is one thing you can do to help another person experience that same grace?

.Here are some ideas to get you started:

- Pray specifically each day for one person you know who would benefit from an encounter with the Lord.

- Share a copy of your favorite faith-centered book with another person. Free and low-cost resources for this can be found at **dynamiccatholic.com**.

- Form a new small group and lead the participants through this study ***Genesis:*** *Seven Life-Changing Encounters with the God of New Beginnings* (Chapters 1-25).

Next Steps

I pray that reading Genesis and sharing in this study have helped you deepen your faith. Even more, I pray that you have encountered the presence of God in a fresh, life-giving way.

As you move forward in your faith journey, continue to use the prayers provided in this Study Guide. In particular, I invite you to make the Dynamic Catholic Prayer Process a part of your daily life.

May Christ Jesus fill your life with abundance, both now and forever. And may you share that good news with the people you know, meet and love.

Grace and Peace,
Allen

> **Man, himself created in the "image of God" [is] called to a personal relationship with God...**
>
> **Catechism of the Catholic Church, 299**

Acknowledgements

Designed By: Hannah Steen

Cinematography By: Claire Arrivo, Tatumn Holland, and Micah Simms

Animation By: Emily Martinez

Special thanks to: Jack Beers, Jenna Greiwe, Mary Joy Kozak,
and Stephen Anderson